easy paper airplanes

Norman Schmidt

STERLING INNOVATION
New York

STERLING INNOVATION
New York

An Imprint of Sterling Publishing
387 Park Avenue South
New York, NY 10016

STERLING INNOVATION and the distinctive Sterling Innovation logo are registered trademarks of Sterling Publishing Co., Inc.

© 2012 by Sterling Publishing Co., Inc.

This book is excerpted from the following Sterling/TAMOS titles:
Best Ever Paper Airplanes © 1994 by Norman Schmidt
Super Paper Airplanes © 1994 by Norman Schmidt

ISBN 978-1-4027-9610-4

This book is part of the *Easy Paper Airplanes* kit and is not to be sold separately.

Distributed in Canada by Sterling Publishing
c/o Canadian Manda Group, 165 Dufferin Street
Toronto, Ontario, Canada M6K 3H6
Distributed in the United Kingdom by GMC Distribution Services
Castle Place, 166 High Street, Lewes, East Sussex, England BN7 1XU
Distributed in Australia by Capricorn Link (Australia) Pty. Ltd.
P.O. Box 704, Windsor, NSW 2756, Australia

For information about custom editions, special sales, and premium and corporate purchases, please contact Sterling Special Sales at 800-805-5489 or specialsales@sterlingpublishing.com.

Manufactured in China

Lot#:
6   8   10   9   7
06/14

www.sterlingpublishing.com

Contents

Flight

People have been obsessed with the idea of flight ever since they looked into the sky and saw birds soaring gently overhead. Mythical stories in many cultures around the world have flying creatures of all sorts, including human beings. When did the reality of human flight begin?

Archeologists in Egypt have discovered a small wooden bird, carved from lightweight sycamore wood, that has a very aerodynamic shape. This small wooden bird is unlike any real bird because its tail has both horizontal and vertical surfaces, just like present-day airplanes. It is not known whether this was a toy, a weather vane, or a small model of some larger craft.

There are other examples of flying toys, such as the Saqqara bird invented by the Greek philosopher Archytas in about 345 B.C. It was a small wooden dove attached to an arm that allowed it to "lift off" in wavering flight. It is not known how the bird was propelled. At about the same time, the Chinese philosopher Mo Tzu constructed what was possibly the first kite, which is simply a tethered airplane. Some Europeans made wings of wood, cloth, and bird feathers, strapped them to their arms, and jumped off high buildings. In 1020, Eilmer "the flying monk" did this, and attained some success with flight, but broke both his legs in the attempt. In the 1500s, the artist and inventor Leonardo da Vinci made many drawings and models of different kinds of aircraft, including the parachute. Another story from the 1700s tells of a French locksmith named Besnier who, with wings strapped to his arms and legs, jumped from a tall building and glided over neighboring houses.

The development of kites continued, and they became the forerunners of free-flying airplanes. European inventors and scientists used them to carry out experiments in aerodynamic forces. Such experiments led to the first free-flying airplanes of Sir George Cayley in the 1790s. They demonstrated the principles of flight as they are understood today. In the 1850s, Sir George's coachman was among the first people to fly in an actual airplane. The stage was now set for the development of controllable airplanes.

Construction

When carefully made, the paper airplanes in this book are super flyers. They can be built using the paper included, or ordinary 20 or 24 lb bond copier paper measuring 6½ inches by 8½ inches (16.5 cm by 21.6 cm). Bond paper is lightweight, easy to cut and fold, and easy to fasten together. It is available in a variety of colors (black paper may have to be purchased at an art store). Since a paper airplane's lift and thrust are limited, every effort must be made to keep drag at a minimum. Every surface not parallel to the direction of travel (wings, nose, and canopy) adds drag, so the neater and more accurate your construction, the better the plane will fly. Clean and accurate cuts and crisp folds are a top priority.

MEASURING AND CUTTING

Use a sharp pencil to mark the measurements and draw firm, accurate lines. Cut out pieces with a sharp pair of scissors or a craft knife and a steel-edged ruler. A knife makes a cleaner cut. When using a knife be sure to work on a proper cutting surface.

FOLDING

Always lay the paper on a level surface for folding. Folding is easier along a score line (an indented line on the paper made with a hard pencil drawn along a ruler). There are only four kinds of folds used in making the airplanes in this book. They are mountain folds, valley folds, sink folds, and reverse folds. Where multiple layers are folded, run your fingers back and forth along the fold, pressing hard to make a sharp crease.

GLUING

A glue stick works well for paper airplanes. Follow the instructions for gluing. Cover the entire contacting surfaces that are to be joined. If there are multiple layers, apply glue to each of the sheets. Glue should be used sparingly, but use enough to hold the parts together. Where multiple layers are being joined, you may need to hold the pieces for a few minutes until the glue sets.

Mountain Fold   **Valley Fold**   **Sink Fold**   **Reverse Fold**

A **MOUNTAIN FOLD** and a **VALLEY FOLD** are actually the same kind of fold. Both are made by folding a flat piece of paper and sharply creasing the fold line. The only difference is that one folds up (valley fold) and the other folds down (mountain fold). They are distinguished only for convenience in giving instructions.

To make a **SINK FOLD**, begin with paper that has been folded using a mountain (or valley) fold and measure as required across the folded corner. Then push in the corner along the measured lines, making a diagonal fold. Finish by creasing the folds sharply.

To make a **REVERSE FOLD**, begin with paper that has been folded using a mountain (or valley) fold and measure as required, down from the top and in from the edge. Then cut along line from the top (heavy line). Push cut piece in, as shown. Finish by creasing folds sharply.

Trimming
for Flight

Air is made up of small, solid, evenly spaced particles called molecules. Everything in the universe is made up of molecules, but air molecules are quite far apart compared with those that make up metal, wood, or paper, and they are easily separated when a body moves through them. The molecules are piled up in a thick layer from the ground, and this is called the atmosphere. It forms part of the space around us and the sky above us. This layer of air molecules (atmosphere) exerts pressure on everything in the world, and it is this pressure that makes flight possible. The shape of the airplane affects the molecules as they move across the airplane's surfaces, increasing or decreasing air pressure, determining the flight characteristics of the plane.

No paper airplanes are perfectly straight. And they are easily bent. Shown on page 8 is an example of trimming using the rudder. Airplane A flies straight

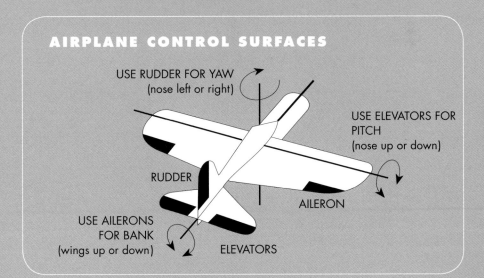

AIRPLANE CONTROL SURFACES

USE RUDDER FOR YAW
(nose left or right)

USE ELEVATORS FOR PITCH
(nose up or down)

RUDDER

AILERON

USE AILERONS FOR BANK
(wings up or down)

ELEVATORS

because air flows smoothly along its surfaces. It needs no trim. Airplane B yaws to its left because the air on the left is deflected by the bent fuselage, increasing air pressure on that side. The rudder is used to compensate. Airplane C again flies straight because it has been trimmed so that the deflected air on the left is opposed by air being deflected by the rudder on the right. But airplane C does not fly as well as airplane A because it is creating much more drag.

Before making any trim adjustments to a paper airplane that you have just constructed, be sure you are releasing the plane correctly for flight. Always begin with a gentle straight-ahead release, keeping the wings level. Hold the plane between thumb and forefinger just behind the center of gravity. As your technique improves, you can throw harder, adjusting the trim as needed. But remember, all planes do not fly at the same speed.

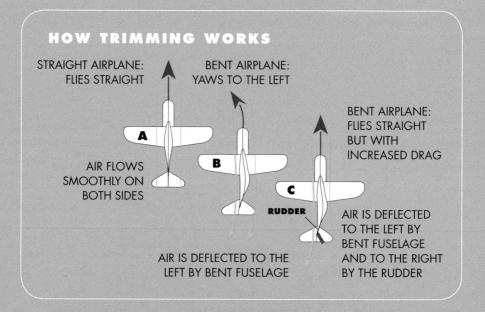

HOW TRIMMING WORKS

STRAIGHT AIRPLANE: FLIES STRAIGHT

BENT AIRPLANE: YAWS TO THE LEFT

BENT AIRPLANE: FLIES STRAIGHT BUT WITH INCREASED DRAG

AIR FLOWS SMOOTHLY ON BOTH SIDES

A

B

C

RUDDER

AIR IS DEFLECTED TO THE LEFT BY BENT FUSELAGE

AIR IS DEFLECTED TO THE LEFT BY BENT FUSELAGE AND TO THE RIGHT BY THE RUDDER

NOTE: Fly Safely. Some of the airplanes in this book have sharp points, so never fly them towards another person. If you fly the airplanes outdoors they may go farther than you expect. Be sure they do not go into the street where you will have to retrieve them.

Flying Tips

Don't be discouraged if on first flight your paper airplane "corkscrews" and crashes. Flying paper airplanes is a delicate balancing act. Only when everything works in harmony—wings, horizontal tail, vertical tail, and control surfaces—is successful flight achieved. With each paper airplane that you build, aim to improve the construction. When carefully made and trimmed, the paper airplanes in this book are super flyers. But remember, the performance of each airplane differs. Experimentation is necessary in order to achieve maximum performance. This is part of the fun of flying paper planes.

Folds that are not neat and crisp add drag to the airplane. This will decrease glide performance. Sloppy folds can also result in twisted airplanes. Inaccurate gluing does not help matters. A twisted plane is sure to "corkscrew" badly (see below). The importance of careful folds cannot be overemphasized.

Airplanes must be symmetrical—one side must be just like the other. On both sides wing and horizontal tail sizes, shapes, and thicknesses must be the same. Also make sure that the control surfaces on one side are the same sizes and are bent the same amount as on the other side.

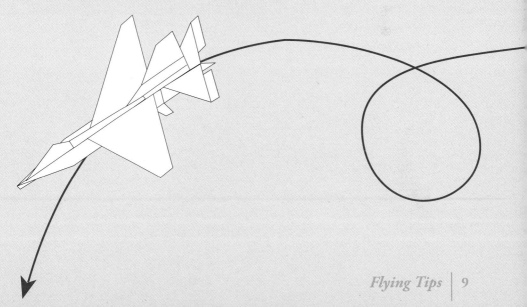

Make sure that the dihedral (upward slanting of wings and tail) is adjusted correctly. In each design, refer to the last step of construction for suggestions. Sometimes experimentation with a different dihedral (or none at all) will be successful. Dihedral provides stability; however, too much dihedral has a destabilizing effect.

Some of the airplanes in this book have secondary control surfaces (flaps). Secondary control surfaces need special attention. If they are bent down slightly, lift is increased. If they are bent down 90°, drag is greatly increased and the nose will pitch down. Additional up elevator is needed, increasing the angle of attack but also increasing drag. Trimmed in this way an airplane does not glide very far. In full-sized airplanes, this trim is good for landing. Experiment with different settings of the secondary control surfaces. Adjust carefully for best results.

Paper airplanes are not baseballs. They cannot be thrown hard. To launch, hold the fuselage lightly between thumb and forefinger near the point where the plane balances. Throw with a firm forward motion, keeping the nose level, pushing the airplane more than throwing it. With a bit of practice you will discover just how hard each of the planes need to be thrown under different conditions.

PITCH TRIM

Although the paper airplanes in this book are built to resemble a bird or powered aircraft, they are obviously all gliders. For thrust they must convert altitude into airspeed. The pitching axis is very important in determining airspeed. Once properly trimmed, an airplane will always fly at the same speed. If the airplane zooms toward the ground, bend the elevators up slightly to raise the nose.

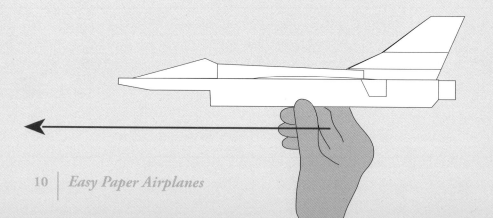

If more speed is needed, as in an outdoor flight, less up elevator will produce the desired result.

ROLL TRIM

Providing the wings are not twisted, the wings should remain more or less level in flight. If one wing drops, bend the aileron down slightly on that wing and up slightly on the other wing.

YAW TRIM

If the plane still has a tendency to turn, bend the rudder slightly opposite to the direction of the turn.

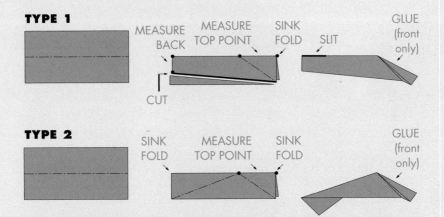

CANOPIES

TYPE 1

MEASURE BACK
MEASURE TOP POINT
SINK FOLD
SLIT
GLUE (front only)
CUT

TYPE 2

SINK FOLD
MEASURE TOP POINT
SINK FOLD
GLUE (front only)

STEP 1 Measure and cut paper to dimensions specified for the particular airplane. Lay paper flat in a horizontal direction. Fold in half horizontally, using a mountain fold.

STEP 2 With the paper folded in half as in Step 1, measure top point and draw lines. For type 1, sink fold (see page 6) the front corner and cut on heavy line. For type 2, sink fold front and back corners.

STEP 3 Press flat to finish the canopy. Only the front end should be glued.

Egret

BACKGROUND INFORMATION

This airplane is called the "Egret" because of its slender shape and long nose. It is a delta (triangle) wing design. The plane looks like a flying triangle. Delta wings are used in slow-flying planes such as hang-gliders and high-speed planes such as the Concorde, which carried passengers faster than the speed of sound. Delta wings will probably be used in future planes that will carry passengers into space and back.

TECHNICAL INFORMATION

The Egret is constructed similarly to the common paper airplane that everyone makes. But because of this model's carefully measured shape, it can attain a very smooth and flat glide. Make sure that its shape is properly adjusted, with vertical tails straight up and down. Hold it between thumb and forefinger, launching it gently straight ahead.

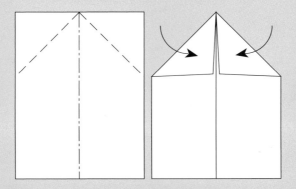

STEP 1 Lay paper flat in a vertical direction. Fold paper in half vertically using the mountain fold. Unfold. Then valley fold the upper corners to the center crease.

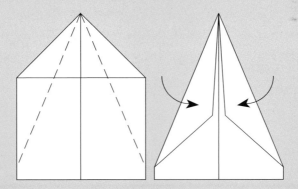

STEP 2 Valley fold the upper diagonals along broken lines to meet the center crease.

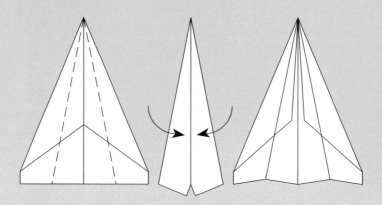

STEP 3 Valley fold outer edges along broken lines to meet the center crease. Unfold, as shown.

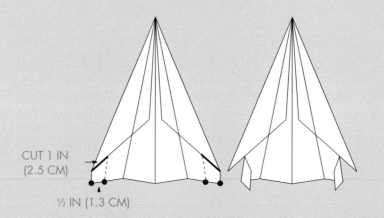

CUT 1 IN
(2.5 CM)

½ IN (1.3 CM)

STEP 4 On each side, measure along diagonal edge of the paper, as shown by heavy line, and cut. Measure along bottom edge, in from each wing tip, and from this point, draw a line to the end of the cut. Valley fold along this line to make vertical tails.

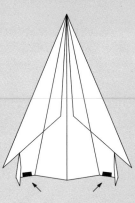

STEP 5 In the locations shown, measure, cut, and fold the elevators.

ELEVATORS ⅜ in x ¼ in (1.0 cm x .6 cm)

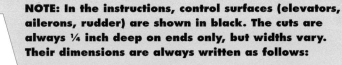

NOTE: In the instructions, control surfaces (elevators, ailerons, rudder) are shown in black. The cuts are always ¼ inch deep on ends only, but widths vary. Their dimensions are always written as follows:

¾ IN x ¼ IN (1.9 CM x .6 CM) OR
⅜ IN x ¼ IN (1.0 CM x .6 CM)

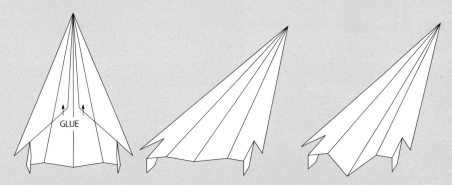

STEP 6 Glue folds only at the center of fuselage. Flip airplane over. Adjust shape so that when viewed from the back, the airplane makes a shallow upside-down W, as shown.

Pipit

BACKGROUND INFORMATION

This airplane is called the "Pipit" because of its small size, just like the bird by that name. This paper airplane has small wings for its weight, which makes it a fast flyer. It can be thrown hard. It is well suited for flight both indoors and out.

The Pipit is a compact little airplane folded entirely from one sheet of paper. It can be constructed without control surfaces. For trimming adjustment, bend the entire airplane. If thrown hard, it will fly not only fast but far. For launching, hold it between thumb and forefinger.

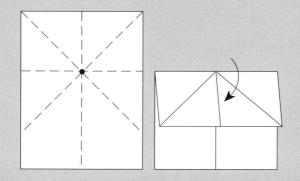

STEP 1 Lay paper flat in a vertical direction. Fold paper in half vertically using a valley fold. Unfold. Then valley fold diagonally so that right upper edge meets the left outer edge. Unfold. Repeat, folding down left upper edge. Unfold. Using the intersection of the creases as a reference, valley fold upper section of the paper along broken horizontal line, as shown.

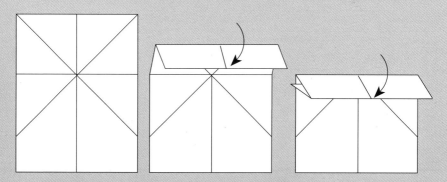

STEP 2 Unfold paper. Valley fold top edge to horizontal crease. Valley fold again along horizontal crease.

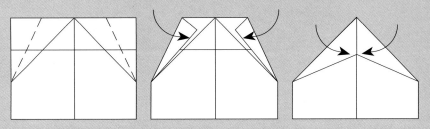

STEP 3 Using a valley fold, bring outer edge to meet the right diagonal crease. Repeat, folding over left edge. Then valley fold the diagonal creases.

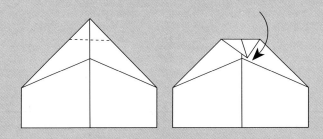

STEP 4 Valley fold tip down to meet crease, as shown.

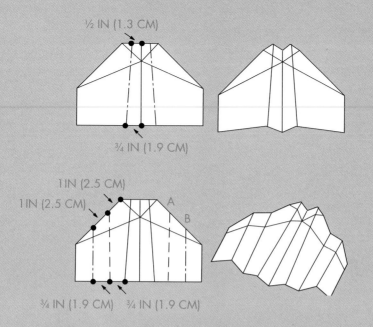

½ IN (1.3 CM)

¾ IN (1.9 CM)

1 IN (2.5 CM)

1 IN (2.5 CM)

A

B

¾ IN (1.9 CM)   ¾ IN (1.9 CM)

STEP 5 On each side of vertical center crease, measure and draw lines as indicated. Then mountain fold along drawn lines, as shown. Measure and draw the next two sets of lines, on each side. Valley fold line A and mountain fold line B on each side, as shown.

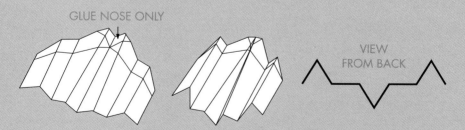

GLUE NOSE ONLY

VIEW FROM BACK

STEP 6 Glue nose only, and let back flare open. Adjust so that, when viewed from back, it makes a shape as indicated.

Swallow

BACKGROUND INFORMATION

This airplane is called the "Swallow" because of its deeply forked tail, which resembles that of the bird. When airplanes were first invented, many different kinds of tails were tried. This is an interesting looking airplane. It can soar in a gentle breeze.

The Swallow is also folded completely from one sheet of paper. It can be constructed without control surfaces. For trimming adjustment, bend the entire airplane. For launching, hold between thumb and forefinger. Launch this airplane gently. Fly it indoors or out.

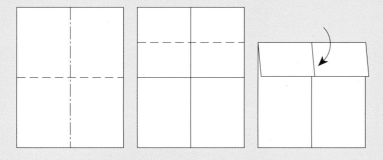

STEP 1 Lay paper flat in a vertical direction. Fold paper in half vertically using a mountain fold. Unfold. Valley fold the paper in half horizontally. Unfold. Then valley fold the top to meet the horizontal crease.

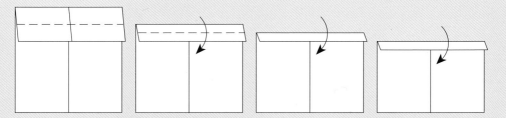

STEP 2 Valley fold the top again to meet the horizontal crease. Then valley fold the top again, to meet the horizontal crease. Finally, refold the original horizontal crease.

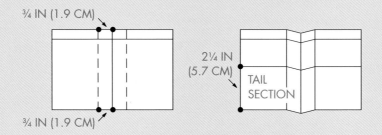

¾ IN (1.9 CM)

2¼ IN
(5.7 CM)

TAIL
SECTION

¾ IN (1.9 CM)

STEP 3 On each side, measure from center crease and draw lines, as shown. Valley fold along these lines. Unfold. Measure from bottom along side and draw a horizontal line.

1⅛ IN   1¼ IN
(2.9 CM) (3.2 CM)

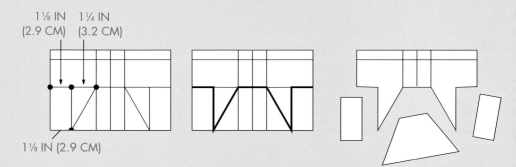

1⅛ IN (2.9 CM)

STEP 4 Measure and draw lines on tail section, as shown. Cut out along heavy lines, as shown. Discard cutouts.

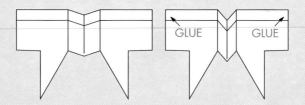

STEP 5 Reshape the airplane by refolding the vertical creases. At each wingtip, glue folded-over portion of the wing's leading (front) edge. Glue no more than ¾ in (1.9 cm) from each wingtip.

STEP 6 Measure, draw, and cut along heavy line at back of fuselage, as shown. Reverse fold to make the vertical tail (see page 6).

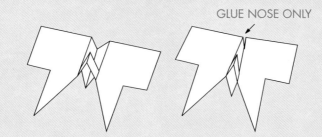

STEP 7 Apply glue to the nose only, leaving the back to flare open. Adjust the wings so they are level in flight.

Condor

BACKGROUND INFORMATION

This airplane is called the "Condor" because of its large broad wings. This design is a variation on a flying wing. Unlike conventional airplanes, this design has no horizontal and vertical tail. Winglets are incorporated into the wingtips, which provide both horizontal and vertical stability. Like all flying wings, it is sensitive to pitch control. The wide wingspan makes it quite fragile, and it should be launched gently straight ahead. It is not a windy weather airplane.

TECHNICAL INFORMATION

Condors have large feathers at their wingtips for control. Instead of feathers, this airplane has winglets. Because of its wide wingspan, this paper airplane is fragile where the wings meet the fuselage. Adjust the winglets and bend the airplane for trim adjustment.

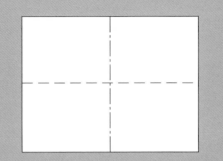

STEP 1 Lay paper flat in a horizontal direction. Fold paper in half vertically using the mountain fold. Unfold. Then valley fold in half horizontally. Unfold.

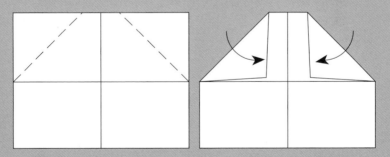

STEP 2 On each side, valley fold diagonally so that the outer edges meet the horizontal crease.

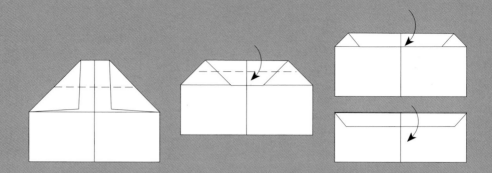

STEP 3 Valley fold along broken lines so that top edge meets the horizontal crease. Valley fold again, so that top edge meets the horizontal crease. Then refold the original horizontal crease.

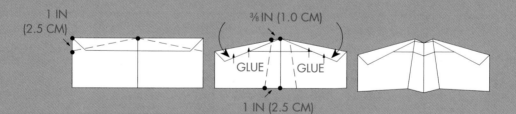

1 IN (2.5 CM)

⅜ IN (1.0 CM)

GLUE   GLUE

1 IN (2.5 CM)

STEP 4 On each side of vertical crease, measure and draw diagonal lines. Valley fold top outer edges along these lines. Glue folded-over triangles to form the leading (front) edges of the wings. Then measure and draw vertical lines, as shown. Valley fold along vertical lines to form the fuselage.

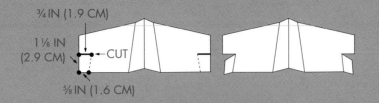

¾ IN (1.9 CM)

1⅛ IN
(2.9 CM)

CUT

⅝ IN (1.6 CM)

STEP 5 Flip the airplane over. On each side, measure and draw lines for the winglets. Make horizontal cuts on heavy lines. Valley fold, as indicated, to make winglets. Make a canopy type 2 (see page 11).

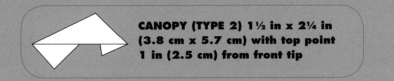

CANOPY (TYPE 2) 1½ in x 2¼ in (3.8 cm x 5.7 cm) with top point 1 in (2.5 cm) from front tip

GLUE
NOSE
ONLY

VIEW FROM BACK

STEP 6 Apply glue to inside of nose only, and insert canopy. Align with nose. Adjust the shape so that the wings have a slight dihedral angle (upward slant) and the winglets slant upward, as shown.

Biplane

BACKGROUND INFORMATION

One way to improve lift without making large wings is having two sets of them, one above the other (biplanes). The box-like construction of these airplanes made it easy to cross-brace the lightweight wooden frames with wire for strength. In 1903, Orville and Wilbur Wright put an engine into a biplane and became the first to attain sustained powered flight. Biplanes were used for most of the air battles of World War I, which began in 1914. Fighter biplanes were highly maneuverable although difficult to handle. Some examples are the Spad 7, Sopwith Camel, and Fokker 7. Biplanes are now used where small, durable, and maneuverable airplanes are required. Crop spraying is a good example. This paper airplane is modeled on early biplanes.

TECHNICAL INFORMATION

Biplanes have stubby noses and short wings and tails, making them sensitive to pitch and roll because the distances from the center of gravity to the control surfaces are small. The planes require careful trimming.

If the airplane zooms nose down to the ground, bend the elevators up slightly to raise the nose in flight.

This may cause the nose of the plane to pitch up sharply. As a result, the air no longer flows smoothly over the wing surfaces but separates into eddies and the wings stall. To solve this problem bend the elevators up less.

If the elevators are not bent at all and the nose still rises, don't bend the elevators down to correct the problem (a plane should never fly this way). Rather add a bit of extra ballast to the nose.

If the plane veers to left or right, bend the aileron up slightly on the wing that rises and down slightly on the wing that falls. Also bend the rudder on the vertical tail slightly, opposite to the direction of the turn.

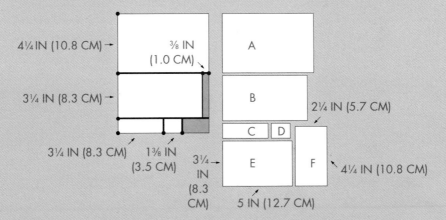

STEP 1 Measure and cut the various pieces from a sheet of bond paper, as shown. Two additional pieces (E and F) are needed, as shown.

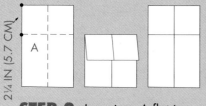

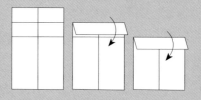

2¼ IN (5.7 CM)

STEP 2 Lay piece A flat in a vertical direction. To make the fuselage, fold in half vertically using a valley fold. Unfold. Measure and valley fold horizontally, as shown. Unfold.

STEP 3 Valley fold the top to meet the horizontal crease. Then refold the original horizontal crease.

VIEW FROM BACK

STEP 4 Valley fold each side so that outer edges meet the center crease, as shown.

STEP 5 Fold each side again using a mountain fold, so that outer edges meet center crease at back. Then adjust folds so that paper looks like an upside-down W, as shown.

GLUE

GLUE

GLUE

STEP 6 Unfold fuselage completely. Refold, applying glue to all contacting surfaces, as shown. Make sure fuselage is straight. Do not glue nose yet.

STEP 7 Lay piece B in a horizontal position to make the lower wings. Fold in half vertically, using a mountain fold. Unfold. Fold in half horizontally, using a valley fold. Unfold. Then valley fold so that top edge meets center crease. Fold again so that top edge meets center crease. Refold original horizontal center crease.

³⁄₈ IN   ⁵⁄₈ IN
(1.0 CM)   (1.6 CM)

1 ¼ IN (3.2 CM)

STEP 8 Unfold completely. On each side, measure and cut diagonally, as shown. Refold. Apply glue before refolding original horizontal center crease only. The folded-over part is the bottom of the leading edge (front) of the wings.

STEP 9 On each side, measure and valley fold, as shown.

STEP 10 Lay piece E horizontally to make the upper wings. Fold in half vertically, using a mountain fold. Unfold. Fold in half horizontally, using a valley fold. Unfold. Then valley fold so that top edge meets center crease. Fold again so that top edge meets center crease. Refold original horizontal center crease.

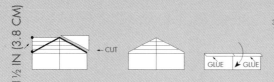

1½ IN (3.8 CM)

← CUT

GLUE | GLUE

⅜ IN (1.0 CM)

⅜ IN (1.0 CM)　1⅛ IN (2.9 CM)

STEP 11 Unfold completely. On each side, measure and cut diagonally, as shown. Refold. Apply glue before refolding original horizontal center crease only. The folded-over part is the bottom of the leading edge (front) of the wings.

STEP 12 On each side of upper wings, measure from each wingtip and mark attachment points for lower wings, as shown. Cut out center piece on trailing edge, as shown. Make ailerons in locations indicated.

AILERONS ³⁄₈ in x ¹⁄₄ in (1.0 cm x .6 cm)

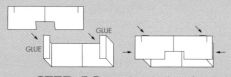

GLUE

GLUE

STEP 13 Applying glue, fasten upper and lower wings together, as shown. Make sure both leading edges face the same direction.

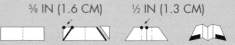

⅝ IN (1.6 CM)　½ IN (1.3 CM)

STEP 14 Use piece C to make the horizontal tail. Valley fold in half vertically. Unfold. On each side, measure from outer edges, as shown, and cut along heavy lines. Then, on each side, measure from center crease and mountain fold, as shown. Make elevators.

ELEVATORS 1 in x ¼ in (2.5 cm x .6 cm)

¼ IN (.6 CM)　⅝ IN (1.6 CM)

STEP 15 Measure and cut leading edge along heavy lines, as shown. On trailing edge, make rudder.

RUDDER ⅝ in x ¼ in (1.6 cm x .6 cm)

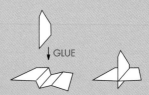

GLUE

STEP 16 Apply glue to inside of horizontal tail and insert vertical tail, aligning trailing (back) edges.

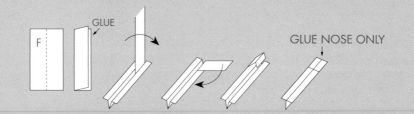

STEP 17 Use piece F to make the nose cowl (ballast). Valley fold piece in half vertically. Glue halves together. Applying glue to one side, insert F into nose and wrap entirely around fuselage, as shown. Then glue fuselage together at nose only.

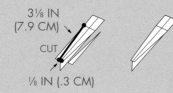

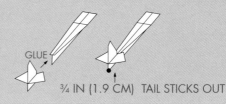

STEP 18 On each side, measure and cut fuselage back along heavy lines, as shown.

STEP 19 Applying glue, slide the tail into the back of the fuselage.

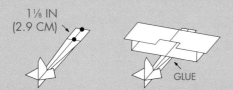

STEP 20 Measure from front of fuselage and mark front of wing position. Glue wings in place, as shown.

VIEW FROM BACK

STEP 21 Measure and cut back of fuselage, as shown. Adjust dihedral (upward slanting of wings and tail) to finish airplane.

X1 Experimental

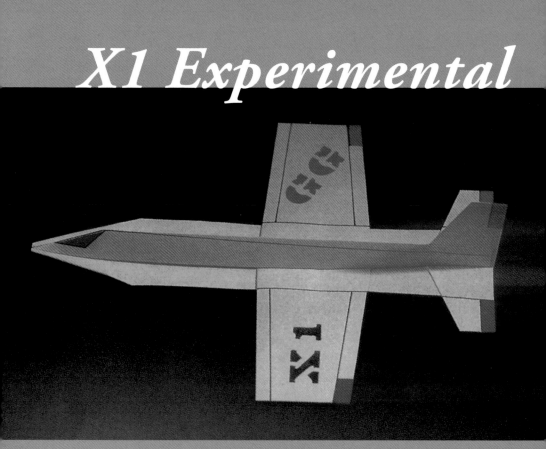

BACKGROUND INFORMATION

Some people believed that the speed of sound was a barrier that would never be crossed. But designers did not abandon their quest. They shaped an airplane like a 50 caliber bullet, which was known to travel faster than the speed of sound. This experimental plane was the stubby-winged Bell X1. It was called "Glamorous Glennis" after the pilot's wife. While this plane did not have swept-back wings, it successfully "broke the sound barrier" for the first time in 1947. Thus began the building of a long series of X planes used for experiments in ultra-high-speed and high-altitude flight.

The X15, for example, flew 8 times the speed of sound to the edge of space at an altitude of 70 miles (112 km) in 1956. This paper airplane is modeled on the Bell X1.

TECHNICAL INFORMATION

What we hear as different sounds are actually differences in air pressure that strike our eardrums. These waves of air (called sound waves) travel at about 760 mph (1,224 kph). An airplane traveling at that speed creates a tremendous pressure ridge because so many air molecules are piled up ahead of its leading edges. What makes it so dangerous is that as speed increases, the ridge of pressure moves farther back over the wings and begins to affect the control surfaces which are on the trailing edges. Airplanes that successfully fly faster than the speed of sound must be designed so that the pressure is deflected in such a way that it does not affect aircraft control. Thus, their noses are pointed and their wings are thin, and either tapered or swept back. The planes must also be built strong enough to withstand the pressure. When supersonic airplanes break the sound barrier, they create a loud booming noise (like a clap of thunder), as heard from the ground.

The speed of sound is also called Mach 1, twice that speed Mach 2, three times Mach 3, and so on, in honor of the scientist Ernst Mach.

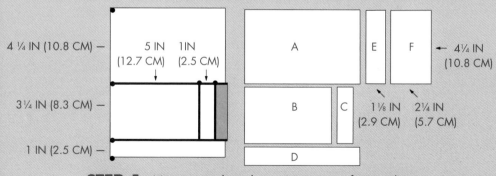

STEP 1 Measure and cut the various pieces from a sheet of bond paper, as shown. Two additional pieces, E and F, are needed, as shown.

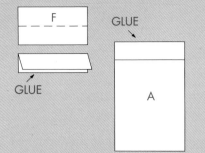

STEP 2 Use piece F to make nose ballast. Lay flat in a horizontal direction and valley fold horizontally. Glue halves together. Then glue to piece A, as shown.

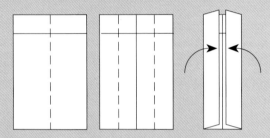

STEP 3 Lay piece A flat in a vertical direction. To make the fuselage, fold in half vertically using a valley fold. Unfold. Then valley fold each side so that outer edges meet center crease, as shown.

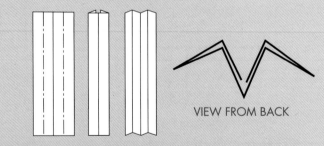

VIEW FROM BACK

STEP 4 Fold each side again using a mountain fold, so that outer edges meet center crease at back. Then adjust folds so that paper looks like an upside-down W, as shown.

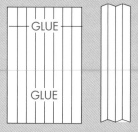

STEP 5 Unfold fuselage completely. Refold, applying glue to all contacting surfaces, as shown. Make sure fuselage is straight.

1½ IN
(3.8 CM)

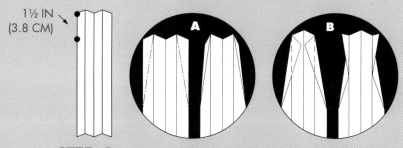

STEP 6 On each side, measure from top (front of fuselage), mark, and mountain fold along broken lines, as shown in enlarged view A. Then flip over fuselage. On each side, valley fold triangle along broken lines, matching fold line to existing crease, as shown in enlarged view B.

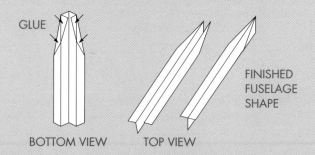

GLUE

BOTTOM VIEW   TOP VIEW

FINISHED
FUSELAGE
SHAPE

STEP 7 Glue triangles. Hold in place until glue sets. It is important that the fuselage stay straight. Do not glue nose yet.

STEP 8 Lay piece B horizontally to make the wings. Fold in half horizontally, using a valley fold. Unfold. Fold in half vertically, using a mountain fold. Unfold. Then valley fold so that upper edge meets center crease. Fold over again along original center crease.

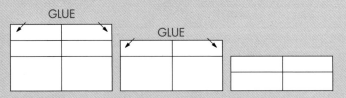

STEP 9 Unfold completely. Refold, applying glue to no more than ¾ in (1.9 cm) from outer tips, as shown. The folded-over part is the bottom of the leading edge (front) of the wings.

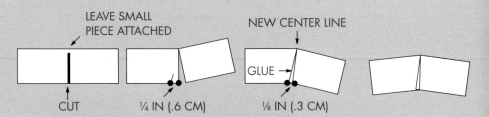

STEP 10 To taper wings, cut along center heavy line from trailing edge (back), leaving a small piece attached at the leading edge. Then measure and make a mark on trailing edge, as shown. Align pieces to the mark. Glue. Measure and draw a new center line.

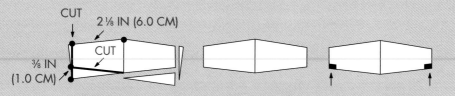

STEP 11 On each side, measure and cut, as indicated by heavy lines. On the trailing edges of wingtips, make ailerons.

AILERONS ⅜ in x ¼ in (1.0 cm x .6 cm)

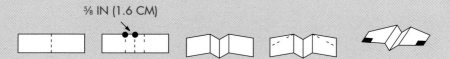

STEP 12 Use piece C to make the horizontal tail. Valley fold in half vertically. Unfold. On each side, measure from center crease, as shown, and mountain fold. On each side, measure and mountain fold leading edge along broken lines. Glue. Make elevators on trailing edges.

ELEVATORS ⅝ in x ¼ in (1.6 cm x .6 cm)

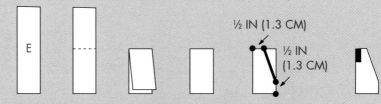

STEP 13 Lay piece E vertically to make the vertical tail. Valley fold in half horizontally and glue halves together. Measure and cut along heavy line, as shown. Make rudder on trailing edge.

RUDDER ⅝ in x ¼ in (1.6 cm x .6 cm)

GLUE

SLIT 1 IN (2.5 CM)

D

STEP 14 Finish the tail. Apply glue to inside of horizontal tail and slide vertical tail in place, aligning at trailing edge.

STEP 15 Use piece D to make the canopy (see page 11). Make slit in the back of canopy.

CANOPY (TYPE 1) 1 in x 6½ in (2.5 cm x 16.5 cm)
Top point 1⅛ in (2.9 cm) — Back is straight

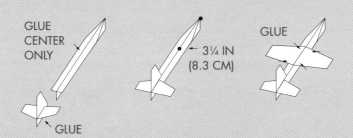

GLUE
CENTER
ONLY

3¼ IN
(8.3 CM)

GLUE

GLUE

STEP 16 Apply glue to inside center only of fuselage. Then apply glue and slide tail into fuselage, aligning at trailing edge. Measure from front and mark for wing position. Glue wings to fuselage.

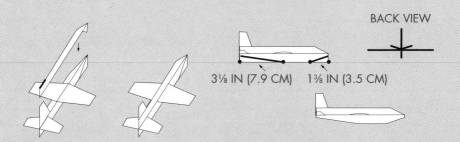

BACK VIEW

3⅛ IN (7.9 CM)   1⅜ IN (3.5 CM)

STEP 17 Apply glue to inside back of canopy and front tab of canopy. Insert tab into fuselage. The vertical tail fits into slit. Align at nose. To finish, measure and cut front and back of fuselage along heavy diagonal lines, as shown. Adjust dihedral (upward slanting of wings and tail).

Nighthawk

BACKGROUND INFORMATION

This airplane is called the "Nighthawk" because it is modeled on the Lockheed F117 Stealth, which is used primarily for nighttime military operations. It is not a fast airplane, but it is highly maneuverable. The unusual shape of the F117, together with its black color, are what make the airplane difficult to see, even by radar. This paper model has fine flying characteristics.

TECHNICAL INFORMATION

This is an unconventional airplane design. For the most realistic appearance, this paper airplane should be made from black paper. This model does not have a standard canopy, and care must be taken in shaping it. The airplane can be trimmed for level flight or aerobatic flight. Fly it indoors or out. For launching, hold between thumb and forefinger.

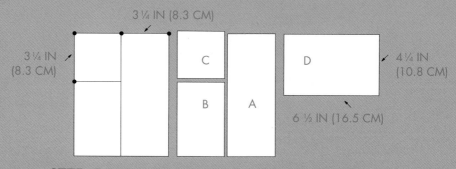

3 ¼ IN (8.3 CM)

3 ¼ IN
(8.3 CM)

C

D

4 ¼ IN
(10.8 CM)

B   A

6 ½ IN (16.5 CM)

STEP 1 Measure and cut three pieces from a sheet of 6½ in x 8½ in (17.5 cm x 21.6 cm) paper. One additional piece is needed, as shown.

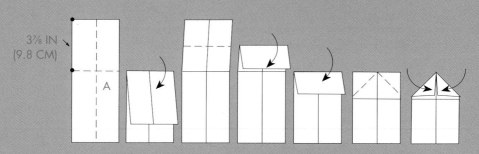

3⅞ IN
(9.8 CM)

A

STEP 2 To make the fuselage, fold piece A in half vertically using a valley fold. Unfold. Measure from top, as shown, and valley fold horizontally. Unfold. Then valley fold so that the upper edge meets horizontal crease. Refold the original horizontal crease. Then on each side, valley fold diagonally so that top edge meets center crease.

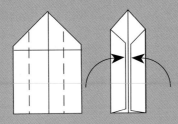

STEP 3 Valley fold each side so that outer edges meet center crease, as shown.

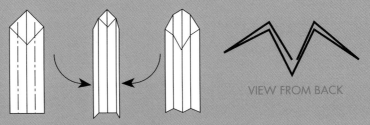

VIEW FROM BACK

STEP 4 Fold again using a mountain fold, so that outer edges meet center crease at back. Then adjust folds so that paper looks like an upside-down W, as shown.

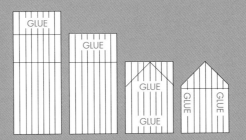

STEP 5 Unfold fuselage completely. Refold, applying glue to contacting surfaces, as shown. Make sure fuselage is straight.

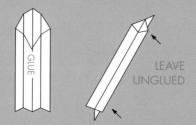

STEP 6 To finish fuselage, glue center of fuselage, leaving 1½ in (3.8 cm) at the nose and ¾ in (1.9 cm) at the tail end unglued.

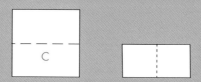

STEP 7 Use piece C to make the twin vertical tails. Fold in half horizontally using a valley fold. Glue sides together. Valley fold vertically. Unfold.

STEP 8 On each side, measure from center crease and mountain fold. Unfold, as shown. On each side, measure and draw lines, as shown.

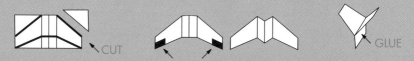

STEP 9 On each side, cut on heavy lines, as shown. Make rudders (see page 15). Adjust creases, as shown, and glue at center.

RUDDERS ⅝ in x ¼ in (1.6 cm x .6 cm)

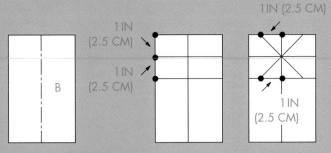

STEP 10 Use piece B to make the canopy. Fold in half vertically using a mountain fold. Unfold. On each side, measure and draw lines, as shown.

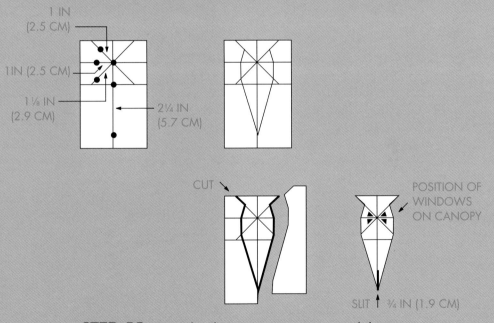

STEP 11 On each side, continue measuring and drawing lines. Then cut along heavy lines to make canopy outline, as shown. Make a slit at the bottom.

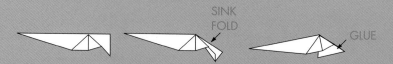

SINK
FOLD

GLUE

STEP 12 To finish canopy, mountain fold along diagonal and horizontal lines. Unfold. Fold again along original center crease, as shown. Then sink fold the front (see page 6). Glue front only.

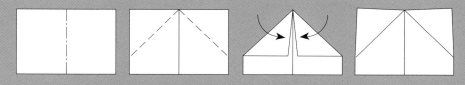

STEP 13 Use piece D to make the wings. Fold in half vertically using a mountain fold. Unfold. On each side, valley fold diagonally so that top edge meets center crease. Unfold.

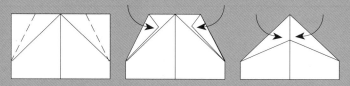

STEP 14 Fold diagonally using a valley fold, so that outer edge meets diagonal creases, as shown. Then fold again along original diagonals.

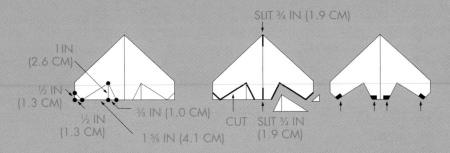

SLIT ¾ IN (1.9 CM)

1 IN (2.6 CM)

½ IN (1.3 CM)

½ IN (1.3 CM)

⅜ IN (1.0 CM)

1 ⅝ IN (4.1 CM)

CUT   SLIT ¾ IN (1.9 CM)

STEP 15 Flip wings over. On each side, measure and draw lines. Cut along lines and make slits at the top and bottom, as shown. Make elevators and ailerons (see page 15).

AILERONS ELEVATORS ⅜ in x ¼ in (1.0 cm x .6 cm)

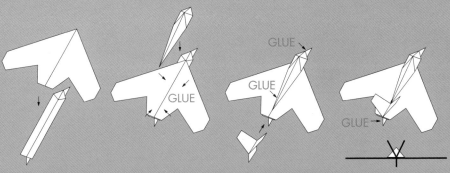

GLUE

GLUE

GLUE

GLUE

GLUE →

VIEW FROM BACK

STEP 16 Glue wings to the fuselage, aligning at the trailing (back) edges. Make sure that the wings are centered and at right angles to the fuselage. To mount the canopy, apply glue to the bottom front tab and the back of the canopy. Slide front tab into the fuselage, aligning with the diagonal front of the fuselage. Make sure the slit at the back of the canopy is centered on the fuselage. Canopy should fit snugly to the wings. Applying glue, slide tail into back of fuselage, aligning trailing edges.

F18 Hornet

BACKGROUND INFORMATION

The F16 was used as a land-based fighter aircraft, but there was no equivalent sea-based fighter. Therefore the F18 was built in the early 1980s as a medium-sized multitask maneuverable military aircraft capable of both sea and land operations. This plane is commonly called the "Hornet." It has tapered wings and a conventional horizontal tail, but with two canted (tilted) vertical tails located between the wings and horizontal tail. The F18 is used by the U.S.A., Canada, Australia, and Spain. This paper airplane is modeled on the F18.

TECHNICAL INFORMATION

The F18 is constructed mostly of aluminum, with parts of its wings and other surfaces made of composites. It has two afterburning turbojet engines that can propel it at almost twice the speed of sound when traveling at high altitudes. This airplane is both a fighter and an attack plane, and it can be fitted with a wide variety of armament for both air-to-air and air-to-ground military tasks. Like the F16, it has a missile rail at each wingtip, with space under the wings for other armament and extra fuel tanks. Besides its military role, this plane is also used as an aerial display airplane at air shows.

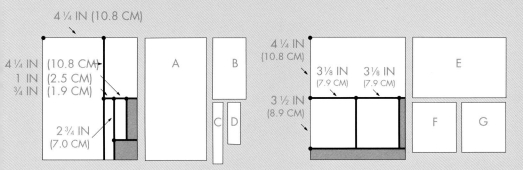

STEP 1 Measure and cut the various pieces from two sheets of bond paper.

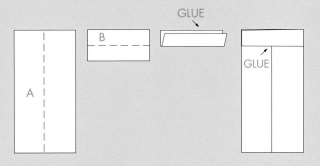

STEP 2 Use piece A to make the fuselage. Fold in half vertically using a valley fold. Unfold. Then valley fold piece B in half horizontally to make nose ballast. Glue halves together. Glue B to A, aligning top edges, as shown.

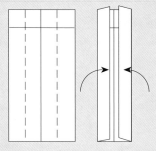

STEP 3 Valley fold so that outer edges meet center crease.

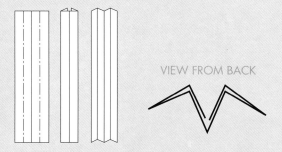

VIEW FROM BACK

STEP 4 Fold each side again using a mountain fold, so that outer edges meet center crease at back. Then adjust folds so that paper looks like an upside-down W, as shown.

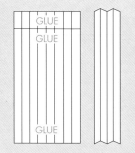

GLUE
GLUE

GLUE

STEP 5 Unfold fuselage completely. Refold, applying glue to contacting surfaces, as shown. Make sure fuselage is straight.

3 ⅛ IN
(7.9 CM)

STEP 6 On each side, measure from top (front of fuselage), mark, and mountain fold along broken lines, as shown in enlarged view A. Then flip over fuselage. On each side, valley fold the triangle along the broken lines, matching fold line to existing crease, as shown in enlarged view B.

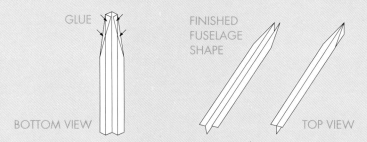

GLUE

FINISHED
FUSELAGE
SHAPE

BOTTOM VIEW

TOP VIEW

STEP 7 Glue triangles. Hold in place until glue sets. It is important that the fuselage stay straight. Do not glue nose yet.

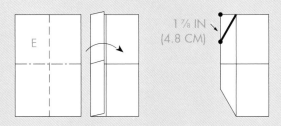

E

1 ⅞ IN
(4.8 CM)

STEP 8 Lay piece E in a vertical direction to make wings. Valley fold in half vertically. Unfold. Mountain fold in half horizontally. Valley fold so that one outer edge meets center crease, as shown. On each side of horizontal center crease, measure and cut diagonally, as shown by heavy line.

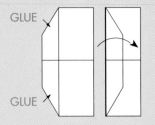

STEP 9 Apply glue to each diagonal side on top layer only, no more than ¾ in (1.9 cm) from the diagonal edge. Refold along the original vertical center crease. The folded-over part is the bottom of the leading edge (front) of wings.

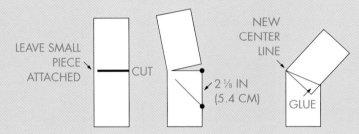

STEP 10 To taper wings, cut along center line from the trailing edge (back), leaving a small piece attached at the leading edge. Then measure and draw diagonal line, as shown. Align halves to the diagonal line. Glue. Draw new center line.

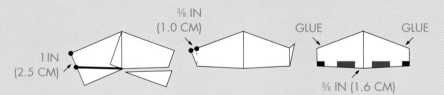

STEP 11 On each side, measure and cut trailing edge, as shown by heavy line. Then on each side, measure and mountain fold wingtips. Glue. Make ailerons and flaps in locations shown.

AILERONS ⅜ in x ¼ in (1.0 cm x .6 cm)
FLAPS 1 in x ¼ in (2.5 cm x .6 cm)

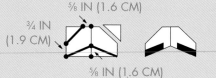

STEP 12
Lay piece F flat in a vertical direction to make the horizontal tail. Valley fold in half vertically. Unfold. Mountain fold in half horizontally. Glue halves together.

STEP 13
On each side, measure and cut, as shown by heavy lines.

ELEVATORS 1 in x ¼ in (2.5 cm x 0.6 cm)

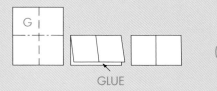

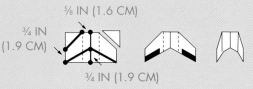

STEP 14
Lay piece G flat in a vertical direction to make the twin vertical tails. Valley fold in half vertically. Unfold. Mountain fold in half horizontally. Glue halves together.

STEP 15
On each side, measure and cut, as shown by heavy lines. Make a rudder on each vertical tail. On each side, valley fold, as shown.

RUDDERS 1 in x ¼ in (2.5 cm x .6 cm)

STEP 16
Use piece D to make the canopy (see page 11).

**CANOPY (TYPE 2) 1 in x 2¾ in (2.5 cm x 7.0 cm)
Top point 1⅞ in (4.8 cm)**

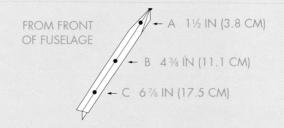

← A 1½ IN (3.8 CM)

← B 4⅜ IN (11.1 CM)

← C 6⅞ IN (17.5 CM)

STEP 17 Measure from front of fuselage, as shown. Make mark A for positioning the front of the canopy, mark B for positioning leading edge of the wings, and mark C for positioning leading edge of the horizontal tail.

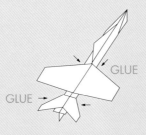

GLUE

GLUE →

STEP 18 Apply glue to the inside of the nose and the small triangles on the bottom of the canopy. Position canopy on the fuselage at mark A. Hold until glue sets. Glue wings and horizontal tail in place, making sure they are centered and at right angles to the fuselage.

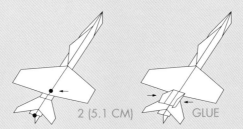

2 (5.1 CM)   GLUE

STEP 19 Measure from back of fuselage, as shown, and make a mark for positioning the twin vertical tails. Glue vertical tails in place, making sure they are centered and parallel to the fuselage.

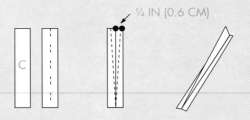

¼ IN (0.6 CM)

STEP 20 Lay piece C in a vertical direction to make the fuselage top. Mountain fold in half vertically. Unfold. On each side, measure and valley fold. Adjust shape, as shown.

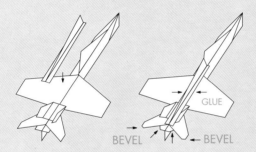

GLUE

BEVEL   BEVEL

STEP 21 Glue piece C onto the fuselage, making sure it fits snugly against the canopy. Bevel the trailing edges of the elevators.

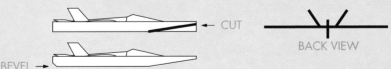

← CUT

BACK VIEW

BEVEL →

STEP 22 Measure and cut nose diagonally, as shown by heavy line. Bevel all corners of the back of the fuselage. Wings and horizontal tail are level. Adjust angles of the canted (tilted) vertical tails, as shown.

Jumbo Jet

BACKGROUND INFORMATION

The first jet-powered airliner was the deHavilland Comet built in the 1950s. As more and more people realized the comfort of jet travel, bigger airplanes were needed to carry them. The Boeing 747 was first built in 1968. It is one of the largest passenger airplanes in the world. It is longer than the distance flown by the Wright brothers (120 ft or 36 m) in their first powered flight. The "Jumbo Jet" is used to carry passengers and cargo across the continents and the oceans of the world. This paper airplane is modeled on the 747.

TECHNICAL INFORMATION

The Boeing 747 is a big airplane. From nose to tail it measures 230 ft (70 m). The distance from wingtip to wingtip is 195 ft (58.5 m). Its tail is 64 ft (19.5 m) high, higher than a five-story building. When it is fully loaded with fuel, passengers, and cargo, it weighs 800,000 lb (360,000 kg), and carries 500 passengers or 270,000 lb (122,500 kg) of cargo. Once it reaches high altitude, it cruises at 600 mph (960 km/h). This makes it ideal for use on long-distance passenger routes. Its service ceiling is 40,000 ft (12,200 m) above the ground. Its maximum range is 6,000 miles (9,600 km), allowing it to fly one fourth of the distance around the earth without refueling. The plane is propelled by four 50,000 lb (22,500 kg) thrust turbofan jet engines.

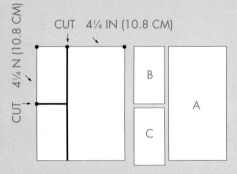

STEP 1 Measure and cut three pieces from a sheet of bond paper, as shown.

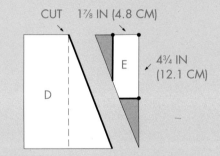

STEP 2 Valley fold a second sheet of bond paper in half vertically. Then measure and cut two pieces, as shown.

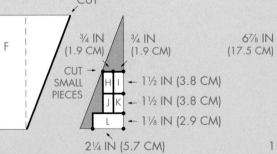

STEP 3 Valley fold a third sheet of bond paper in half vertically. Then measure and cut six pieces, as shown.

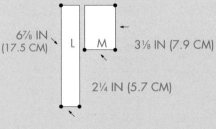

STEP 4 Measure and cut two additional pieces, as shown.

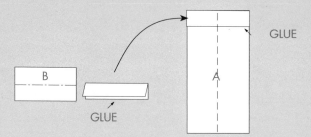

STEP 5 Use piece B to make the nose ballast. Fold in half horizontally using a mountain fold. Glue halves together.

STEP 6 Use piece A to make the fuselage. Glue ballast to the top of fuselage, as shown. Fold in half vertically using a valley fold. Unfold.

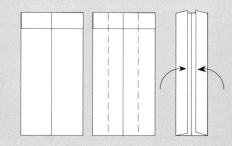

STEP 7 Valley fold each side so that outer edges meet center crease, as shown.

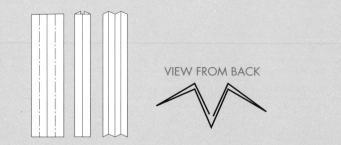

STEP 8 Fold each side again using a mountain fold, so that outer edges meet center crease at back. Then adjust folds so that paper looks like an upside-down W, as shown.

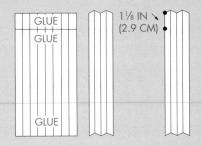

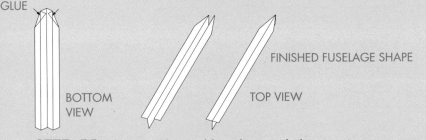

STEP 9 Unfold fuselage completely. Refold, applying glue to contacting surfaces, as shown. Make sure fuselage is straight.

STEP 10 On each side, measure from top (front of fuselage), mark, and mountain fold along broken lines, as shown in enlarged view A. Then flip over fuselage. On each side, valley fold triangle along broken lines, matching fold line to existing crease, as shown in enlarged view B.

GLUE

BOTTOM VIEW

FINISHED FUSELAGE SHAPE

TOP VIEW

STEP 11 Glue triangles. Hold in place until glue sets. It is important that the fuselage stay straight. Do not glue nose yet.

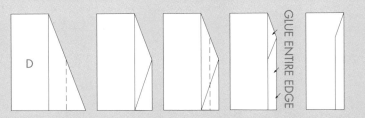

D

GLUE ENTIRE EDGE

STEP 12 Lay piece D vertically to make the right wing. Valley fold vertically so that bottom outer edge meets center crease. Valley fold vertically again so that outer edge meets center crease. Apply glue. Then fold over again along original vertical center crease.

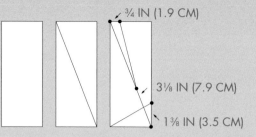

¾ IN (1.9 CM)

3⅛ IN (7.9 CM)

1⅜ IN (3.5 CM)

STEP 13 Flip over, with folded-over edge to the LEFT. Draw diagonal line from upper left to lower right corners. Measure along line from bottom and make a mark. Measure along top edge from left and mark. Join the two marks. Then measure along right edge from bottom and mark. Join this point with the bottom left corner.

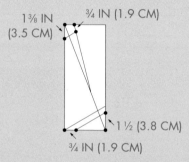

1⅜ IN (3.5 CM)

¾ IN (1.9 CM)

1 ½ (3.8 CM)

¾ IN (1.9 CM)

STEP 14 Measure along left edge from top and make a mark. Measure along line from top, as shown, and make a mark. Join the two marks. Then measure along bottom edge from left and make mark. Measure along right edge from bottom and make a mark. Join marks.

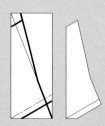

STEP 15 Cut along lines, as shown. Then valley fold along line, as shown.

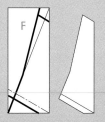

STEP 16 To make the left wing, repeat steps 12–15 using piece F, keeping the folded edge on the RIGHT and reversing the directions of the lines from left to right, as shown.

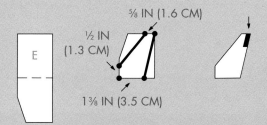

⅝ IN (1.6 CM)

½ IN (1.3 CM)

1⅜ IN (3.5 CM)

E

STEP 17 Lay piece E vertically to make the vertical tail. Valley fold in half horizontally and glue halves together. Then cut along heavy lines, as shown. Make rudder on trailing edge.

RUDDER ¾ in x ¼ in (1.9 cm x .6 cm)

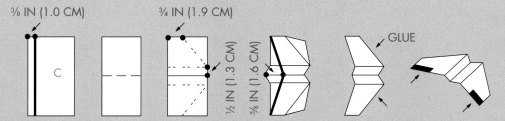

⅜ IN (1.0 CM)

¾ IN (1.9 CM)

½ IN (1.3 CM)

⅝ IN (1.6 CM)

GLUE

C

STEP 18 Lay piece C vertically to make the horizontal tail. Measure and cut to size. Valley fold in half horizontally. Unfold. On each side, measure from center crease, as shown, and mountain fold. On each side, measure and mountain fold leading edge along broken lines. Glue. Cut trailing edges and make elevators.

ELEVATORS 1 in x ¼ in (2.5 cm x .6 cm)

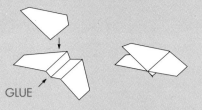

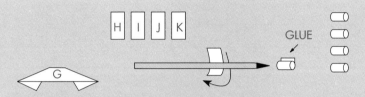

STEP 19 Apply glue to inside of horizontal tail and insert vertical tail, aligning leading (front) edges.

STEP 20 Use piece G to make the canopy (see page 11). Use pieces H, I, J, and K to make the engines. Wrap each piece around a pencil vertically and glue.

CANOPY (MODIFIED TYPE 2) ¾ in x 2¼ in (1.9 cm x 5.7 cm) with top points 1 in (2.5 cm) from front and back tips

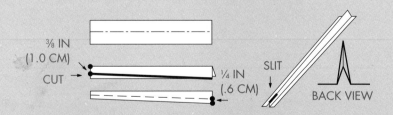

³⁄₈ IN
(1.0 CM)

CUT →

¼ IN
(.6 CM)

SLIT
↓

BACK VIEW

STEP 21 Use piece L to make the top of the fuselage. Mountain fold in half horizontally. Measure and cut as shown. Then, on each side, measure and valley fold to form piece, as shown. Cut a ¾ in (1.9 cm) slit along center crease at narrow end.

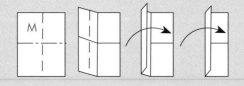

STEP 22 Use piece M to make a spar (support) for the wings. Valley fold in half vertically. Unfold. Mountain fold in half horizontally. Unfold. Then valley fold vertically so that outer edge meets center crease. Fold over again along original vertical center crease.

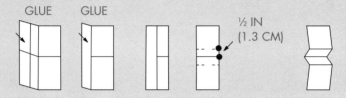

STEP 23 Unfold spar completely. Refold, applying glue to contacting surfaces. Flip over. On each side of center crease, measure and mountain fold, as shown. Folded-over edge is the front.

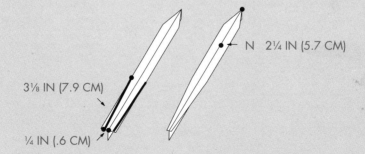

STEP 24 Measure back of fuselage and cut, as shown. Then measure from front and make mark for positioning leading edge of wings at N.

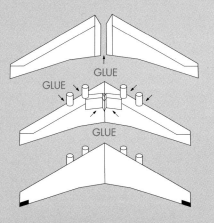

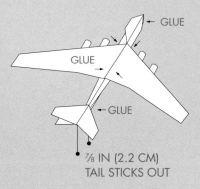

7⁄8 IN (2.2 CM)
TAIL STICKS OUT

STEP 25 With wings upside down, glue halves together. Glue spar to wings. Glue engines to wings in approximate positions shown (they stick out 3⁄8 in (1.0 cm)). Flip over. On trailing edges, make ailerons.

Ailerons 5⁄8 in x 1⁄4 in (1.6 cm x .6 cm)

STEP 26 Apply glue to inside of fuselage, the small triangles on the bottom of canopy, and the center bottom of wings. Slide canopy tabs into fuselage aligning with front tip. Immediately slide wings in place. Then apply glue and slide tail into back of fuselage. Hold until glue sets.

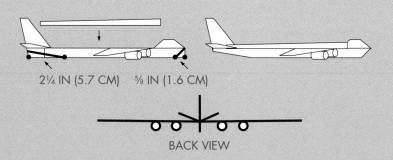

2¼ IN (5.7 CM)   5⁄8 IN (1.6 CM)

BACK VIEW

STEP 27 Measure and cut nose and tail ends diagonally along heavy lines, as shown. Glue L onto top of fuselage, as shown, fitting snugly against back of canopy, with vertical tail through the slit. Adjust dihedral (upward slanting of wings and tail), as shown.

TAV Concept

BACKGROUND INFORMATION

We are living on the threshold of a new era in air travel. Already the space shuttle is blasting into space attached to a rocket and returning as an airplane for another mission. The next generation of space planes will take off under their own power from ordinary airport runways, fly into space, and return back to earth. They are called transatmospheric vehicles (TAVs). Sometimes they are called hypersonic transports (HSTs). They will combine jet and rocket engines for propulsion and have stable delta wings (triangle shaped) integrated into the fuselage for lift in the lower atmosphere. They will look something like the ordinary "paper plane." One example is NASA's experimental X30. This paper airplane is modeled on such future space planes.

TECHNICAL INFORMATION

Transatmospheric vehicles will need powerful and complicated engines and fuel supplies if they are to fly from the ground up into space. It takes a great deal of energy to propel an airplane beyond the limits of the earth's atmosphere and go into space orbit at 22 times the speed of sound. For example, the space shuttle we have now uses over 1,000,000 lbs (450,000 kg) of liquid oxygen and 300,000 lb (135,000 kg) of liquid hydrogen, which it burns in less than ten minutes of flight. The fuel is carried in large external tanks, which are thrown away during each flight. Future TAVs will carry everything onboard, like a regular airplane. In addition to engines for very high altitudes, they will also have engines that can burn fuel using oxygen from the atmosphere at lower altitudes. Only at very high altitudes, where there is not enough oxygen in the air to use, will they switch to an onboard supply of oxygen. Space planes of the future will use less fuel and carry much less oxygen. Such planes will be able to fly completely around the world in just a few hours.

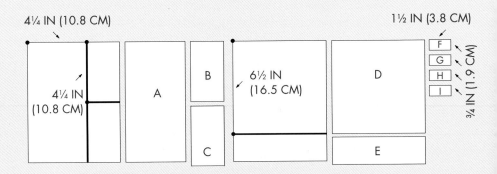

STEP 1 Measure and cut the various pieces from two sheets of bond paper. Four additional small pieces are needed, as shown.

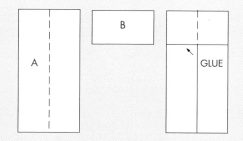

STEP 2 Lay piece A flat in a vertical direction. To make the fuselage, fold in half vertically using a valley fold. Unfold. To make nose ballast, glue piece B in place, aligning the top edges, as shown. Refold center crease. Unfold again.

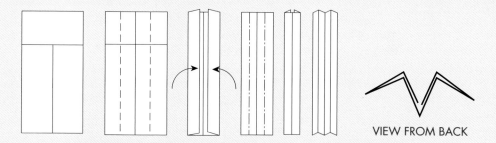

VIEW FROM BACK

STEP 3 Refold in half vertically using a valley fold. Unfold. Valley fold each side so that outer edges meet center crease, as shown. Fold each side again using a mountain fold, so that outer edges meet center crease at back. Then adjust folds so that paper looks like an upside-down W, as shown.

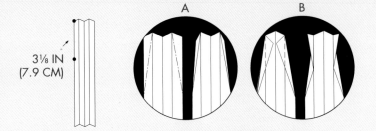

3⅛ IN (7.9 CM)

A B

STEP 4 On each side, measure from top (front of fuselage), mark, and mountain fold along broken lines, as shown in enlarged view A. Then flip over fuselage. On each side, valley fold the triangle along the broken lines, matching fold line to existing crease, as shown in enlarged view B.

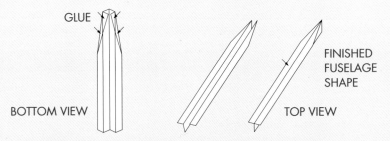

GLUE

BOTTOM VIEW

FINISHED FUSELAGE SHAPE

TOP VIEW

STEP 5 Glue triangles. Hold in place until glue sets. It is important that the fuselage stay straight. Glue fuselage in the middle only, leaving the nose and tail ends unglued.

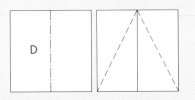

D

STEP 6 Use piece D to make the wings. Mountain fold in half vertically. Unfold. Then on each side valley fold diagonally along a line running from the top center to the bottom corners. Unfold.

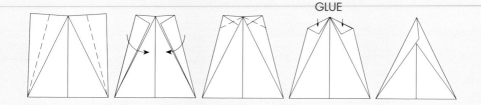

STEP 7 On each side, valley fold diagonally so that outer edges meet diagonal crease, as shown. Then fold so that upper edges meet diagonal crease, as shown. Apply glue to the small upper triangles only and refold original diagonal creases.

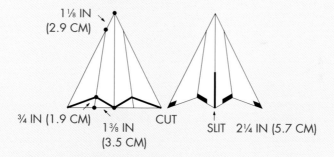

1⅛ IN (2.9 CM)

¾ IN (1.9 CM)   1⅜ IN (3.5 CM)   CUT

SLIT   2¼ IN (5.7 CM)

STEP 8 Lay wings flat, right side up. On each side, measure from front tip and back center and draw lines, as shown. Then cut wings, as shown by heavy lines. Make elevators and ailerons in locations shown. At the trailing (back) edge, cut a slit along center crease, as shown.

AILERONS ⅝ in x ¼ in (1.6 cm x .6 cm)
ELEVATORS ¾ in x ¼ in (1.9 cm x .6 cm)

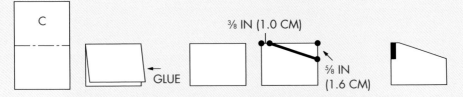

STEP 9 Mountain fold piece C in half horizontally to make the vertical tail. Glue halves together. Measure and cut, as shown by heavy line. Make rudder, as shown.

RUDDER ¾ in x ¼ in (1.9 cm x .6 cm)

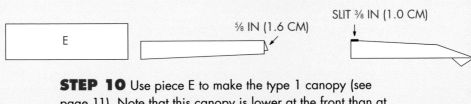

STEP 10 Use piece E to make the type 1 canopy (see page 11). Note that this canopy is lower at the front than at the back. Cut paper to size first.

CANOPY (TYPE 1) 2¼ in x 6½ in (5.7 cm x 16.5 cm)
Top point 2¼ in (5.7 cm), Front ⅝ in (1.6 cm)

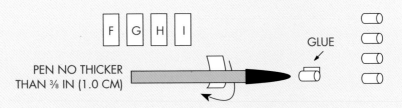

STEP 11 Use pieces F, G, H, and I to make the engines. Wrap paper around a felt-tipped pen vertically and glue.

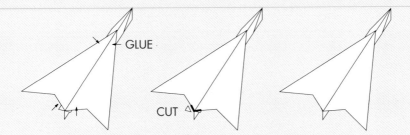

STEP 12 Glue wings to the fuselage, aligning trailing (back) edges. Make sure wings are centered and at right angles to the fuselage. Then trim back of fuselage to match wing trailing edges.

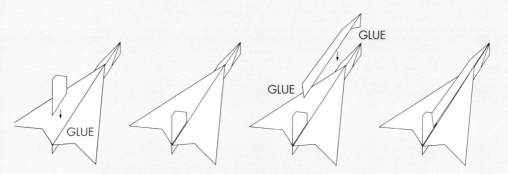

STEP 13 Apply glue and slide vertical tail into fuselage (and the slit in the wings). Align at trailing (back) edges. Apply glue to the lower front tab of the canopy and the inside back. Position canopy by inserting tab into nose end of the fuselage and slipping the back over the vertical tail.

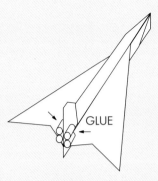

STEP 14 Attach the engines by gluing them to the vertical tail, two on each side, one on top the other, as shown. Align to the trailing edge of the vertical tail.

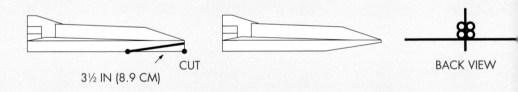

3½ IN (8.9 CM)   CUT   BACK VIEW

STEP 15 Measure and cut nose diagonally, as shown by heavy line. This plane has no dihedral.

Decoration

The following pages contain a plan (top) view and sometimes also an elevation (side) view of most paper airplanes contained in this book. They have window outlines, outlines of control surfaces, and other lines that help define each plane's shape, all of which add to an airplane's realism. Decorative patterns add interest.

The patterns can be copied, modified, or you can invent your own. A pattern such as a checkerboard or a camouflage that is shown on one plane can easily be applied to another airplane design. Use your imagination! What you see here are suggestions. Or you can build paper airplanes and leave them undecorated. You may wish to build undecorated trial planes first so you can master their construction and flight before you spend a lot of time on decoration.

It is easier to add decoration to the airplanes before they are completely assembled. Some advance planning is needed. Once you have decided on the pattern or design you want for the plane, decorate the pieces as you cut and fold them. Try each piece for fit and mark it carefully as you go along. Armament can be added to military planes using toothpicks. Draw the decoration lines using a very fine black felt-tipped pen. Narrow colored markers are ideal for filling in. Avoid water-based markers because they wrinkle the paper too much. Stencils can be used to add numbers and letters.

See the photographed airplanes for ideas on color schemes. Some of the patterns may be different from those shown here.

Egret *See page 12 for color suggestions.*

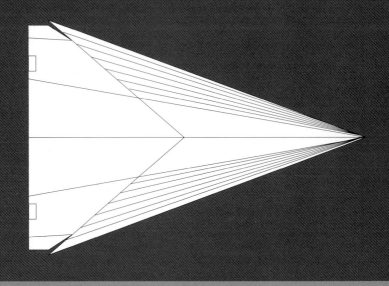

Pipit *See page 16 for color suggestions.*

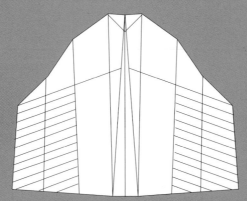

Swallow *See page 20 for color suggestions.*

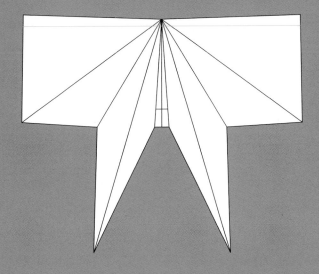

Biplane *See page 28 for color suggestions.*

X1 Experimental
See page 34 for color suggestions.

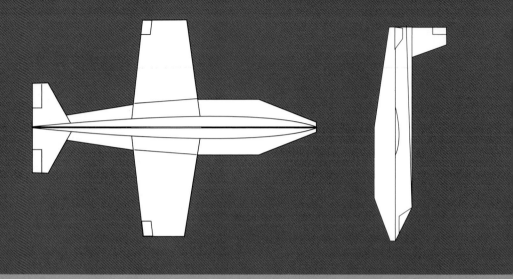

Nighthawk
The Nighthawk has no decoration. It is all black. To add detailing, draw lines (in pencil on black paper) to indicate the engine covers. Add windows to the canopy (see page 45). Also refer to the photograph on page 41.

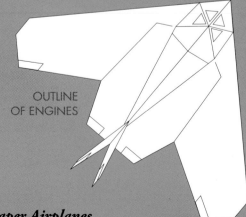

WINDOW
OUTLINE ON
CANOPY

OUTLINE
OF ENGINES

F18 Hornet

See page 48 for color suggestions.

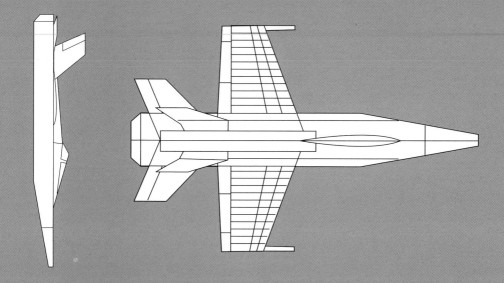

Jumbo Jet

See page 56 for color suggestions.

TAV Concept

See page 65 for color suggestions.

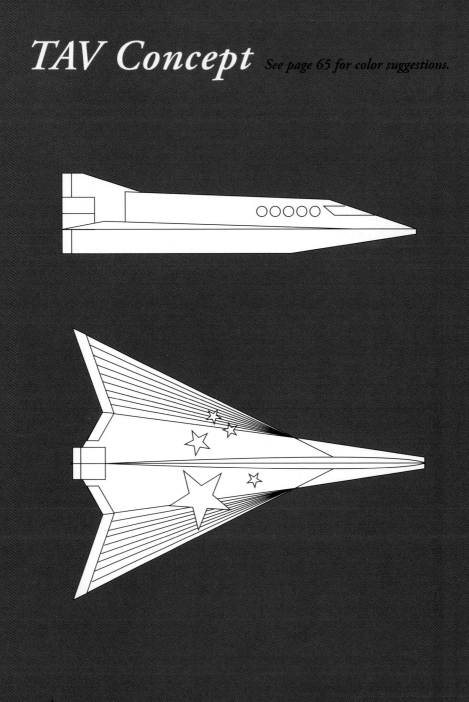

Glossary

ANGLE OF ATTACK The downward slant, from front to back, of a wing.

ANGLE OF BANK The raising of the outside wing and lowering of the inside wing during a turn.

ASPECT RATIO The length of a wing in relation to its width. The longer a wing, the higher its aspect ratio.

ATTITUDE The direction an airplane is pointing in relation to the horizon (banking, yawing, or pitching).

BALLAST Extra weight needed in the nose of an airplane to make the center of gravity coincide with the wings, which provide the lift.

CONTROL SURFACES Small surfaces that can be bent to alter the airflow and change an airplane's attitude—ailerons for bank, elevators for pitch, and rudders for yaw.

DIHEDRAL ANGLE Upward slanting of wings away from the fuselage. (Downward slanting is called anhedral.)

DRAG The resistance of air on moving objects, slowing them down.

FUSELAGE The body of an airplane.

LEADING EDGES The front edges of wings, tails, or other parts.

LIFT The force of air pressure beneath the wings buoying up an airplane.

MANEUVER Skillfully making an airplane fly in a desired direction—turn, climb, dive, stall, spin, or loop.

PITCH Nose-up or nose-down attitude.

ROLL Rotation along the length of an airplane.

SPAR The main internal frame that supports the wing.

STRAKES Wedge-shaped extensions of the wing's leading (front) edges near the fuselage.

TRAILING EDGES The back edges of wings, tails, or other parts.

TRIM Making small adjustments to the control surfaces to affect the attitude of an airplane.

TRIM DRAG The drag (resistance) produced from bending control surfaces into the airflow.

VENTRAL FIN A small stabilizer on each side of the fuselage underneath the tail.

WING LOADING The amount of weight a given area of wing is required to lift.

YAW Nose-left or nose-right attitude.

Index